Fifty Years Of
Ice Cream Vehicles
1949-99

written by

Stuart Whitby & Alan Earnshaw

and based on ideas by
Peter Earnshaw and Bryan Whitby

Trans-Pennine Publishing

Contents

Front Cover: *The old and the new, a 1957 Morris JB with a Bristol Motor Body conversion of an ex-GPO Telephones van stands alongside a new Whitby-Morrison Transit in September 1999. Ade Davies*

Rear Cover Top: *The Ford Thames 307E with Martin Walter bodywork as supplied to Walls Ice Cream in 1964.*

Rear Cover Bottom: *The latest Walls branded Transit, of the type built for special events. Ade Davies*

Title Page: *The fleet of Lenas Ice Cream from Longport, Staffs., with a Morris J 1477cc van, two Bedford CA 1594cc vans, and an Austin A40 Devon 1200cc van. ICA*

This Page: *This Morris Commercial, with its distinctive coachbuilt body (and sliding doors) was operated by Jenkins of Kingston, and is pictured alongside the River Thames. Kevin & Margaret Donovan Collection*

Opposite Page: *Nine Commer-Karrier vans stand outside the Smith's factory in Gateshead, and form part of a delivery to Mr. Softee in Belgium. ICA*

The **Nostalgia Road** Series ™
is conceived, designed and published
by

Trans-Pennine Publishing Ltd.

PO Box 10
Appleby-in-Westmorland
Cumbria, CA16 6FA
Tel. 017683 51053 Fax. 017683 53558
e-mail trans.pennine@virgin.net
(A Quality Guild registered company)

Reprographics
Barnabus Design & Repro
Threemilestone, Truro
Cornwall, TR4 9AN
01872 241185

And Printed in Cumbria by
Kent Valley Colour Printers Ltd.
Shap Road Industrial Estate
Kendal, Cumbria LA9 6NZ
01539 741344

With the kind support of
Whitby Morrison
Crewe, Cheshire CW1 6TT
01270 581318

© Trans-Pennine Publishing 1999
Photographs: Whitby Morrison, The Ice Cream Alliance (ICA), or As Credited

Ice Cream Vehicles - A Foreword

There can scarcely be a man, woman or child in Britain who would not be reminded of happy times when reading this book. Indeed there will be very few who cannot recall the sound of ice cream van chimes, a cold ice in the warm sun, special treats on days out with the family to the park or the seaside, or just running out to the van in the street. We have all stood at the window of an ice cream van, gazed at the pictures of the lollies and ice creams and carefully made our choice. We have felt dwarfed by the ice cream man standing high in his van as he carefully hands us our cornet drizzled with strawberry sauce. It is an experience which is all about pleasure.

The unique vehicles that have brought this pleasure to our home, or to the places we like to visit, are part of the fabric of our society and they deserve the recognition this book gives. Over the past 50 years, the sale of ice creams from vehicles (otherwise known as mobiling) has become a very sophisticated and professional sector of a billion pound industry. This book explains how both the vehicles and the way they operate has changed over the years and gives us an intriguing glimpse over the counter into the world of the ice cream man.

Lisa Greene

Chief Executive
Ice Cream Alliance

Introduction

It is quite strange how the ideas for new publications come about, but in transport publishing few books will have ever begun life quite like this one. Nor, dare I venture to suggest, will many have been originated by a dual father-son team, at least not quite in the way that this one has. The subject itself is also unique, for never before has the subject of mobile ice cream vending been covered in a general release publication. The unique features continue, as this is also the first NOSTALGIA ROAD book to feature a section of colour pages.

Not only has this been done with the use of some remarkable colour images from the period concerned, but it has been achieved with the inclusion of 12 extra pages without any increase in the cover price whatsoever. Regular readers of the NOSTALGIA ROAD series will no doubt appreciate this as an unexpected bonus, but those readers from the world of ice cream mobiling will recognise the name of the company who have generously made this inclusion possible and been highly supportive with the project. I therefore wish to record a debt of thanks to Whitby Morrison who have also kindly sponsored the colour section of this book.

Quite how this book came about is also unique, for it was the idea of my 11-year old son Peter. Now if this sounds like a proud father talking I trust you will forgive me, but the idea was genuinely his! It came one wet, blustery January day when, without being prompted by the chime of an ice cream mobile, he walked up to me and said 'Dad, why don't you write a book on ice cream vans?' Now other than a passing knowledge I really had no idea where to begin, so I dismissed the subject in a rather off-handed manner.

Yet, on second thoughts it was not such a silly idea at all, in fact (and being a self-confessed ice cream addict), it was quite a good suggestion. After all, who does not love ice cream, but how much do we take for granted the vehicles that deliver it from door to door. Furthermore, from an engineering point of view, the vehicles employed in this work present a fascinating subject in their own right, especially with regard to the high standards of coachbuilding. The liveries used on these vehicles (the majority of which are traditionally hand painted by signwriters), also set them apart from the run of the mill commercial vehicles.

The idea went a little further when I was judging at a commercial vehicle rally in the spring of 1999, and I decided to wander across the showground in search of refreshment. There was the usual array of vending vehicles and trailers, but one in particular caught my eye. It was an old Morris J type, which had a queue somewhere twice as long as a brand new Transit a few hundred yards away. Torn between an interest in the old Morris, and the lack of bodies waiting at the Transit, I took the easier option. On seeing my judges badge the vendor in the new Transit, despondently commented that he thought that I would have gone to his competitor's van. I explained my shortage of time, and he looked quite relieved, and said 'whenever I come to one of these vehicle rallies and that chap's there, people will always go to him before me.' I felt quite sorry for him, but I understood what he was saying - the Nostalgia draw of the old J Type was very strong, and it was certainly getting the right market audience even though it was probably nowhere near as efficient as its modern counterpart. On my way home from the show I was more convinced than ever that Peter had a good idea. After all, even the most grizzled and antiquated vehicle enthusiasts have, at some time in their distant past, been children.

Thinking back to my own childhood in Huddersfield, I vividly recall a small family firm had a parlour just across from my Auntie May's house in Milnsbridge. If I was lucky, or had been well-behaved (or not actually caught being naughty), I would get one cornet a week. Ice cream day was usually a Wednesday. If it was warm we'd slink off down to the banks of the Huddersfield Narrow Canal just below the parlour, take our shoes and socks off and dabble our feet in the green slimy water. No thought of tetanus, rusty prams, or goodness knows what else, we were at the seaside or on some tropical island, and ice cream in hand, we were in heaven!

Left: *This line up of vehicles at the 1964 Ice Cream Alliance exhibition is typical of the period but changes were shortly to take place, and the third van from the right already employs the new Whitby direct drive system. From right to left we see an Austin Mini, three Bedford CALs (the first of which is a Fish & Chip mobile) and an Austin LD, all with Cummins bodies. ICA*
Below: *This 30cwt Austin LD carries the Economica soft-ice van body from the Motor Delivery Co. in Northallerton. This firm supplied both Treats and Mr. Really Good. ICA*

When I was ten I caught scarlet fever pretty badly (probably as a result of paddling in the canal), and I ran a high temperature for much longer than normal. Our family GP suggested that ice cream would be a big help, although sadly he did not put it on prescription. Accordingly my mother would go out several times a day and bring some back in a bowl. It was a red hot summer, and we had no fridge in those days, and where she fetched it from I have no idea, but there it was. After a few days I was getting a bit fed up of the stuff, and wanted ice lollies instead. 'No' came the reply, 'ice cream is a food and good for you, lollies are nothing but coloured water and sugar!'

My father came to the rescue, and he looked up from his newspaper and showed us an advert for a new lolly with an ice cream centre - Lyons Maid had brought out something called the Mivvi. I just had to have one, but they were so new that none were to be had anywhere. The fever got worse as the heatwave increased, and day after day my obsession with the Mivvi grew. In the end, and with great flourish, the manager of our local Co-operative store, Eric Sykes, came rushing along our backyard one day with a brown paper bag containing a Mivvi. He said he was keeping the rest of the box in his fridge (just for me) until I was better.

That is my pedigree on the subject, but it is no basis on which to write a book. In fact other than a reasonable knowledge of the various chassis employed by the bodybuilders over the years, I had little idea where to begin. Undaunted by my lack of knowledge, Peter came in one afternoon holding the newly-delivered Yellow Pages. It was opened at the Ice Cream section, and he looked at me and said 'Why don't we write to some of these firms Dad?' 'Alright' I said, 'we will give it a try, but let's just write one letter and give it to Mr. Slee (our local ice cream mobiler) when he comes round on Sunday night.'

So a letter was written and duly handed over, but it was the start of the season and we heard nothing for a few weeks, until a 'phone call was received one Wednesday evening. It was Christopher Slee, with a suggestion that we ought really to try and develop the subject by talking to The Ice Cream Alliance and Whitby Morrison of Crewe. The former being the official body of the ice cream vending industry, the latter being the principle builder of ice cream vehicles today. A point of contact was established with the Whitby's, and their sales manager Dudley Brierley suggested that we send down a few sample copies of the NOSTALGIA ROAD books for them to look at. He seemed very non-committal, so other work took precedence and the package sat around for a few weeks before it was sent. Even then it was only posted after Mr. Slee suggested that we really should get on with it, because Dudley was wondering what had happened as they had heard nothing since our initial (exciting) enquiry.

Top Left: *Talking of Huddersfield and memories, I recall a good friend of mine (Norris Baptiste), leading me along Bentley Street one Friday night in the 1960s to a new ice cream parlour that had just opened up in what once had been Lockwood Town Hall. This was the firm of Dixons, and it holds warm (or should that be cold memories) for Stuart, as one of his first jobs with Whitby's was to install a custom manufactured ice cream display in Dixon's shop.*

Bottom Right: *The fact that this book was written owes much to Christopher Slee from Winskill near Penrith, so it is important to mark his help with this picture of their post-war mobile, an Austin A40 with a body by Lancasters of Carlisle, which is seen here with a group of customers in the village of Murton near Appleby in Westmorland. Christopher recalls that his father built his very first mobile, based on pre-war Morris chassis. Slees of Winskill.*

For many years I have had a desire to produce a book on ice cream vans and had already built up a large collection of material to be included. When Alan first made contact, Dudley (who was fully aware of my wishes) was professionally cautious in his initial reaction. At that time we did not know this was to become a working partnership and more likely a long term friendship. The simple reality was that Alan's vast knowledge of the motor industry and his publishing experience would combine nicely with my knowledge of ice cream vehicles and my passion for the industry.

My involvement with ice cream began at the age of seven, when my mum took me along to an annual Ice Cream Alliance conference at Harrogate. My dad had attended these conferences since the early 1950s, initially in conjunction with S C Cummins Ltd. and later in his own right. For me it was an exciting experience, with all those colourful ice cream vehicles to look at and of course lots of ice creams to eat! This visit to an ICA conference was to become the first of many but because the venue changed each year, it was only possible for me to attend those within 'daytrip' distance.

From then on my interest developed and I spent many weekends and school holidays at my dad's factory. It was here that I learnt the basics of general vehicle construction and refrigeration engineering and the highlight of this work experience being of course testing the soft ice cream machines. My working career began as an engineering trainee at Rolls Royce Motor Cars, but I soon realised that the ice cream industry was my true destiny. I knew that it was only a matter of time before I would be a contributor to it.

Many years have passed and my enthusiasm for this industry is now best described as a passion. This is an industry, which is like no other, and it should be remembered that it is likely that every member of the population has bought ice cream from an ice cream van at some time in their life!

I am now proud to be included as a part of this industry. There is a feeling of satisfaction when meeting a delighted owner of a Whitby Morrison vehicle, and this goes beyond the demands of commercial business. The knowledge that our vehicles are likely to last for at least 20 years and, in time, serve ice cream to hundreds of thousands of people gives me a great deal of pride. The foundations for today's industry were clearly laid by the early mobilers, especially those, whose vision in the 1950s and early 1960s developed the market. That was the time of rapid expansion and everyone from the 'one man, one van' operators to the large franchise operations made an important contribution. We should also recognise the many vehicle body builders and engineers who responded with tremendous innovation to the demands of this rapidly expanding market. This book is my tribute to all of them and is recognition of their contribution to today's society.

Finally I should say that where we have quoted original prices in our text, we have used the Central Statistics Office Retail Price Index, and (in brackets) we show what it would cost you to purchase the item in 1999. We hope that this will help the reader gain an impression of how, despite ever-increasing prices, in real terms some things have stayed pretty much the same or actually become cheaper.

Above: *From an early age Stuart Whitby found himself attending many ice cream conferences along with his father Bryan, who had to attend first on behalf of Cummins and then to demonstrate his direct drive system. The family had to go along too, so Stuart and his two sisters Julie and Diane spent a good deal time enjoying the free samples!*

Below: *The Whitby family is recognised for undertaking many challenging projects, as we will later discuss. This is one such project, which called for a 6x6 Land Rover conversion for a client in South Wales. It now operates on the Pendine Sands, the place where Sir Malcolm Campbell achieved his first world speed record.*

The origin of ice cream is a topic that has been the subject of much speculation over the years, so we asked Josef Boni (President of the Ice Cream Alliance for 1998-9) to clarify what is fact and what is fiction. He writes; 'Legend has all sorts of fanciful stories about Marco Polo bringing ice cream from China, Catherine de Medici introducing it to France, and King Charles I having his own personal ice cream maker. All wonderful stories, but sadly there is not a scrap of historic evidence to back up any of these legends. Marco Polo did not introduce either ice cream or pasta to Europe and worse still, he may never even have been to China. Most of the myths surrounding ice cream seem to have been introduced by the Victorians.

The earliest evidence of anything approaching ice cream being made was in China in the Tang period (A.D. 618-907). Buffalo, cows and goats milk was heated and allowed to ferment. This yoghurt, was then mixed with flour for thickening, camphor (yes camphor!) for flavour and refrigerated, before being served. King Tang of Shang had a staff of 2,271 people which included 94 ice-men. Early freezing of foods was achieved by mixing salt with ice, which reduces the freezing point and makes it quite easy to achieve temperatures lower than -14°C. Just who discovered this process is unknown, but it probably was the Chinese.

We know that the process was discussed in papers written in India in or around the 4th century and the first technical description of ice making, using various salts, was by the Arabian medical historian Ibn Abu Usaybi (A.D. 1230-1270). But the process did not arrive in Europe until around the 16th century, probably being introduced to Italy in 1503. However it was not used for food until water ices (sorbets) appeared in Naples, Florence, Paris and Spain in the 1660s. However, *Tacitus* (the Roman historian) records the use of crushed ice flavoured by wine and syrup, but this may have been more of a drink than a sweet. But by 1664, ices made with sweetened milk had begun to appear in Naples.

In this country Iced Cream, was served at a banquet for the Feast of St. George at Windsor Castle in 1671. Yet it was such a rare and exotic dish that only the guests on King Charles II's table had one plate of white strawberries and one plate of iced cream. All the others had to watch and marvel at what the Royal table were eating. Such was the interest and demand for ice cream that wealthy people built ice houses on their estates. Ice, farmed in winter from lakes, ponds and rivers, was stored below ground in special 'ice-houses' under straw and bark until the summer when it was used for cooling drinks, making water ices and iced creams.

Left: *This Morris Cowley with an 11.9hp engine dates from 1929, but was converted by a firm of carriage builders from South Molton for the Hocking family in 1935. Despite having a fleet of modern Whitby-Mercedes vans, the Cowley remains Hocking's flagship and is still in regular use today!*

Right: *The most common ice cream vehicles were from Bedford. The first successful model was the CA, and this was followed by the CF van in 1969, two of which are seen in this 1978 line up of Scotts vehicles.* ICA

Below: *This Austin LD was produced as a soft-ice van for Laevaggi's of Denton (Manchester) by local builders Kirkbys of Denton. Seen in 1963, it has already done two years in service according to the sign 'Pride in Craftsmanship', which is displayed by the front off-side wheel. Just beyond the LD can be seen a new Karrier 2-ton walk-thru van.* ICA

The ice was of such a poor quality that it was never actually put in food, and was only ever used to chill or freeze food and drinks. Ice cream making was a closely guarded secret and the knowledge of how to make it would have been a meal ticket for life, which is why the first recipe in English did not appear until 1718.

In the 19th century, ice cream manufacture was simplified with the introduction of the ice cream machine in 1843 in both England and America. This consisted of a wooden bucket that was filled with ice and salt and had a handle which rotated. The central metal container, containing the cream was surrounded by the salt and ice mixture. This churning produced ice cream with an even, smooth texture. Previously it was made in a pewter pot kept in a bucket of ice and salt and had to be regularly hand stirred and scraped from the side of the pewter pots with a paddle, which is a sort of miniature spade on a long handle.

The key factor in the manufacture of ice cream was ice and where it could be obtained? By the early 19th century the importation of ice from Norway, Canada and America had started, and this made ice cream readily available to the general public here in the UK. Ice was shipped into London and other major ports and taken in barges down the canals, to be stored in ice houses, from where it was sold to ice cream makers.

This burgeoning ice cream industry, run mainly by Italians, started the influx of workers from southern Italy and the Ticino area of Switzerland to England. In London they lived in the most atrocious conditions in and around the Holborn area. Huge ice house pits were built near Kings Cross by Carlo Gatti in the 1850s, and here he stored the ice that had been shipped to England from Norway. They are still there and have recently been opened to the members of the public visiting The London Canal Museum.

In the late 19th century Gatti was the first to sell ice cream to the masses in England and he established a network of cafes and salesmen with barrows all over the capital to purvey his freshly frozen products. The 'Penny Lick', an ice served in a small glass (which was handed back to the vendor) became popular - even if this method left a little to be desired in terms of hygiene! Things improved when the first ice cream cones became available around the turn of the century.

Over the next two decades many small ice cream concerns were established, often run by Italian immigrants, but the next major revolution to hit the UK ice cream industry was in 1922 when T Wall & Sons began making ice cream on an industrial basis. Made from pure cream and ripe fruit juices in a hygienic Model Factory, their products were sold by grocers and restaurateurs all over London and from a fleet of trikes, due to which the catch phrase, STOP ME AND BUY ONE, was coined. Another major supplier grew from the small chain of shops and corner cafes run by Joseph Lyons & Co., who also began selling dairy produce and ice cream at an early stage.

By the 1930s, nationwide distribution was established and both industrial and artisanal ice cream production thrived in the UK until wartime rationing limited the availability of ingredients. Following World War II, the use of vegetable fat to make ice cream became common and still continues today although manufacturers are required to distinguish between products made of dairy fat and vegetable fat on the packaging or at point of sale. Ice cream was more widely available than other types of confectionery during this period and the UK was established as one of the major ice cream consumers in Europe, despite its climate.

The manufacturing process developed throughout the 1950s and 1960s and ice cream became, and remains, a very safe food following the introduction of heat treatment regulations in the late 1950s. These regulations prescribed temperatures and times for the pasteurisation (or sterilisation) of mix and for subsequent cooling and storage. Industrial production of branded products was dominated by Birds Eye-Walls and Lyons Maid and these companies also ran considerable mobile sales operations.

The next major period of innovation for the UK industry was the 1990s when new players and products abounded. The introduction of the Mars ice cream range and many other products based on popular confectionery countlines helped to boost adult consumption of impulse ice cream, as did the arrival of several so called premium, brands of bulk ice cream. Own label manufacture grew progressively as over half of all ice cream sales became 'take home' products from supermarkets. Walls maintained its dominant position in the branded sector, but Lyons Maid foundered being sold first to the ill fated Clarke Foods and subsequently to Nestle. On a national basis, the branded impulse sector consisted of Walls, Nestle, Mars and the ex-Unilever subsidiary Treats. Other suppliers held only fragments of the market. However, even a fragment could be significant as the industry reached a value of £1billion and the average per capita UK consumption at the end of the 20th century is 8 litres'.

Above: *Taken in July 1961 this picture shows UAN 749 a Smith-bodied Commer supplied as fleet No. 105 to the Mr. Tasty organisation. Routes Group official picture, courtesy ICA*

Top Left: *This line up of Morrison-Electrofreeze vans on the Bedford CA chassis, was taken at the Buxton show of the Ice Cream Alliance in 1968. ICA*

Below: *Three Archibald Scott mobiles on display in 1982, from left to right we see a Bedford CF, a Freight Rover (British Leyland Sherpa) and a Ford Transit L100, the price of the middle vehicle is £7,000 or about £16,000 at today's price. ICA*

The Story Of Ice Cream Mobiling

The popularity of ice cream was so extensive that it was not long before enterprising individuals got the idea of taking the product to the customer instead of waiting for the customer to come to them. This did not diminish the activity of the ice cream parlours (and in fact increased them if anything), but rather created a genuine increase in the trade, and effectively copied the dairy industry.

The dairying industry had been doing delivery of milk from door to door for many years. This delivery service had started as a product of the first industrial revolution, which began during the reign of Queen Elizabeth I, when Britain's towns and cities began to increase in size. Hitherto even the city centres had never been far from open countryside with its cows, dairy produce, eggs, fresh meat and vegetables. But as the cities grew in size, pressure was placed on the availability of 'fresh food' supplies, as a result we find what is probably the oldest city dairy in the world being opened at the Strand in London during Stuart times (probably around 1640), with a shop on the site following soon after.

With the exception of the 'Royal' cows that were kept in the city's Royal Parks, those animals that were used to supply milk for the populace spent their lives in byres with poor lighting and ventilation. They were in fact little more than diseased battery conditions, and the industry was neither precise, hygienic or reliable. The cowmen also had problems in balancing demand, so in some parts of the city there might be a surplus, but in other parts a drought.

The milk itself was distributed in iron pails (often rusty), which were pushed around in perambulators or carried on horse drays. The containers (usually without lids) were open to dust, germs, and often trailed along not very far from the rear end of a horse. Dishonest dairymen were known to water down the milk, and it is recorded that 'there were complaints when small fish were found swimming in the household delivery.' In an 1852 issue of *Punch,* it was said that 'a clean glass of milk would be one of the seven wonders of London.' With regard to cream it was even worse, as it is reported that thickening was achieved with the use of snail slime!

As the industrial revolution of the 19th-century grew, Britain became increasingly urbanised, and it became the first country in the world to do so. Milk, the staff of life, was essential, but improvements in supply had to be made. In 1840 milk was being sent by rail from the Cheshire countryside to top-up the Manchester dairies, and the technique followed in other cities. It was still a haphazard service, and it was not until George Barham began his services to London in 1864 that there was any real organisation. Barham called his firm the Express Country Milk Supply Company (now known as the Express Dairy).

Even though he found that he was balancing supply and demand quite well, Barham was often left with surplus supplies, and as this would not keep he looked for ways to sell it on to firms that could process the milk. Butter was one process, but the most important need was a means of keeping the milk cool and fresh. In the chilling of milk, Barham borrowed technology from the brewing industry in the form of 'capillary cooling'. With good, clean supplies now coming into London (from as far away as the Yorkshire Dales and the West Country), milk could be sold to retail outlets. The trade through these shops was brisk and profitable, but Barham reckoned, why sell to other outlets when you could have your own dairy shops. Others copied the dairy shop concept, including the Aerated Bread Co. and a small tobacconist partnership known as Joseph Lyons!

The role that Barham played in assisting Lyons develop their cafes and dairy shops is not widely known, nor is the fact that he was intimately concerned with another well-known high street name of today - Sainsbury's. In fact Barham almost persuaded Sainsbury to sell his shop to the Express Dairy, and thereafter become the company's Provisions Manager. Yet it is with the surplus supplies of milk (which the Express Dairy made available to the ice cream industry) that we are most intimately concerned. By the 1870s the Express were bringing in to London upwards of 30,000 gallons of country milk each night. Most of this went through the shops, or was delivered door to door by the Express 'roundsmen' who, between them, were covering 300,000 miles a year on their deliveries.

Yet there was still a great degree of surplus, but this surplus varied from day to day. Butter producers were looking for constant supplies, and the dairy firms were meeting this demand from their daily quota. The problem was what to do with the occasional peaks in available milk, for having brought it all the way to London, Victorian thrift baulked at pouring the unwanted residues down the drain. It is said that Titus Barham, who had a great liking for ice cream met an Italian ice house owner called Granelli at a social event, and between them a deal was struck over the surplus milk supplies. Thereafter when it was converted into ice cream, the milk's life was prolonged and all parties were happy!

Another Brick From The Walls: *The traditional face of the ice cream seller between the two world wars, is pictured here with this view of a Walls 'Stop Me & Buy One' trike. These tricycles were introduced to sell ice creams and lollies in 1922, after Walls found that retailers would not co-operate by stocking their products. The same type of 'vehicle' was also used to deliver the company's meat products to shops. The system was highly successful and by 1936 it had even been exported to the Rock of Gibraltar. Motor transport was also used, mainly for delivery, as shown by the Ford Model TT below.* Birds-Eye Walls

"T.T.F.N."

It's ta-ta for now to station tea wagons — or most of them — but when railway travel becomes more normal again, PASHLEY will be ready with new types — designed and built in the light of PASHLEY'S wide war-time experience.

Every PASHLEY vehicle is designed by specialists and constructed by craftsmen. Each is a leader in its own field. Remember the name PASHLEY. . . .

Left: *In this book we have tried to incorporate some period advertisements reflecting the changes in mobiling after the war. Their overall condition is not good, but they do show what was happening in the period concerned. This one by Pashley was produced in 1944, and it reads 'It's ta-ta for now to station tea trolley - or most of them, but when railway travel becomes more normal again, PASHLEY will be ready with new types - designed and built in light of PASHLEY'S wide war-time experience.*

Above: *In 1946 the Southern Railway began introducing tea trolleys once again, and this new type also carried an ice cream container, in addition to the tea urns and cake stands.*

Above Right: *A relatively typical post-war mobile is seen here with this Cummins-bodied Morris J that was produced in 1952 as a Mobile Ice Cream Shop for a Mr. M. E. Brewer of Rathbone Road, Liverpool 13.*

Bottom Right: *An advert for the Favourite Ice Biscuit Co. Ltd., London E7 in December 1944 reads: 'The Curtain Rises! Ice cream is on the stage again, its return greeted with applause - and now, what of your cones and wafers. There never was better value than "Favorite" Cones and Wafers. A reputation of 55 years for unquestionable quality and value - good materials blended with skill - evenly baked - wholesome and crisp. They make satisfied customers. A word of Advice. Customers will be kept supplied to the best of our ability and to enable us to make equal and fair distribution kindly assist us by placing your orders long before delivery is required.*

The availability of extra milk supplies, at a marginally reduced cost substantially increased production and in turn this provided the impetus for the start of the mobiling trade. It is clear from the records of the Express Dairy Company, that this mobiling trade started in Britain a good ten years ahead of the American 'Hokey-Pokey' carts, but it is equally clear that once the Americans started, they quickly overtook the British retailers.

Ice cream had been taken to the USA in 1774 by a London confectioner named Lenzi and it was significantly developed following the introduction of Nancy Johnson's hand-cranked freezer in 1846. The freezer was further developed by a Mr. Young in 1848, and within two years a Canadian, Thomas Webb, had started a successful ice cream vending business in Toronto. The following year Jacob Fussell began commercial production at Baltimore, Maryland and he went on to become known as the 'Father of the American Ice Cream Industry'. Between these characters, the spur to the industry was assured, and as ice cream went from luxury food to popular 'treat', mobile vending began in great seriousness.

The handcart or the tricycle were the most common means of mobiling up to the war, and motor vehicles were a luxury rather than being commonplace. To mix metaphores we might say that 'Antonio's Ice Cream Cart Ruled - OK'. The vendors using motor vehicles were generally those aiming at event trading, especially where events were some distance from their parlour or cold store. The vehicles were often second-hand, but with new coach built bodies added to them. Cabinets containing the ice creams etc. were generally insulated with cork, although block ice and dry-ice types were also common. The main problem in these being the need to sell the produce before the temperature rose sufficiently enough to allow thawing. For this reason motorised vending became crucial when attending distant events, as it was unreasonable to expect the horse and cart or trike mobiles to cover a long journey, and still have the contents in a frozen state late in the day.

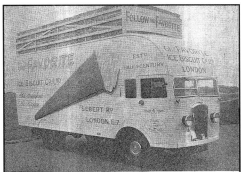

That the day of the motorised ice cream vehicle was coming we can clearly see, but some readers may wonder why we have chosen 1949 as the starting point of this account. The answer is simple, for although motorised ice cream vehicles had been around from the early days of motoring, the big boom was not to take off until after World War II. The reason for this was two-fold, first of all many of the carts, trikes and vehicles that had been employed in vending before the war had been requisitioned for other uses, largely milk delivery. Secondly the vendors themselves had faced a mixed bag of fortunes some being interned, others joined the armed forces, many others went into directed employment including the NAAFI service. Neither was it a time for luxury, and rationing impacted heavily on the industry, so it was largely put on hold for the 'duration'.

Of course ice cream vending continued throughout the war, but only in a limited fashion, and the business was therefore ripe for a complete overhaul on the resumption of peace. It is obvious that the new means of vending would centre on motorised vehicles, but in view of the vehicle shortages it is also clear that the ice-cream business was given a low priority when it came to new vehicles!

The industry was gearing up to new beginnings, but it seemed as though officialdom was against it from the start. This was most notable in the form of new vehicle allocation. However, it is not hard to understand why, for at the time a chronic shortage in commercial vehicle chassis existed, and we can see just how serious this was by the fact that old army lorries were being re-bodied for use in applications as important as ambulances and fire engines. In light of the chronic shortages, a confidential list of priority allocations were given to the main manufacturers, and it included almost every conceivable trade or profession, 326 of them in all - including Vendors of Ices, Minerals & Confectionery. The one presented to Bedford Motors listed this category of customers second from the bottom, only purveyors of rags and bones came lower. Some new chassis did find there way into the trade though, and it may well be that (as both mobile shops and mobile snack bars came in the top 100) some dealers were liberal in their application of the Ministry regulations. For the majority of ice cream businesses the chance of a new motor was pretty slim, and as a consequence firms like Pashley, Raleigh, Triumph and BSA strongly promoted the delivery bike.

However, 'new' ice cream vans did seem to be in evidence, but in reality these were little more than new bodies on an old chassis. The records show that a large number of pre-war London taxis were sold for re-bodying when new taxis (number 12 on the priority list) became available in 1946-7. Accordingly the ice cream trade began to see 62hp Ford V8s, and Vauxhall DX saloons having ice cream bodies fitted. Actually that statement implies there was a standard ice cream van body, but it was anything but. In fact you simply took along your chassis to the local coach builder and asked him to put on a body that suited you. Robert Pascalli recalls, 'we went along and asked a firm called Hinds in Carlisle for a suitable conversion to our 10hp Ford CX, and he had no idea what to do. After a bit of thought he said, "how about I make it like that one there, but give you extra headroom"; the that to which he pointed was an Austin that they had just built with a hearse body. When it came it was just what we wanted, a spacious kiosk on wheels, and he had even used the same type of etched glass windows he had put in the hearse!' This situation was fairly typical, as local builders produced ice cream vans using traditional techniques, ash frames and sheet metal or wooden sides. There was no speciality, and the next vehicle in the workshop might be a removal van, a bus or even another hearse!

Top Left: *An example of a pre-war ice cream vehicle, whcih is either a Ford Model A or an Austin 12, both of which would date from the late 1920s. ICA*

Bottom Left: *A late Model-T Ford used by A. Borza & Son in Airdrie, Scotland - it would probably date between 1926 and 1928.*

Top Right: *A Fordson E83W bodied for Matley's by Cummins in 1953.*

Centre Right: *The first postwar advert for an ice cream mobile was placed by Hendersons in 1949, but it was their first and last advert.*

Bottom Right: *This Fordson E83 is seen at the Cummins factory with Roy Andrews, Derek Bennion and Barry Walker around 1952/3.*

17

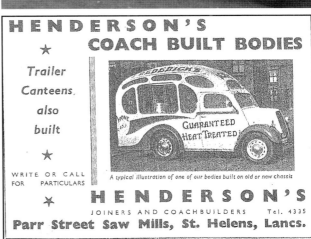

HENDERSON'S COACH BUILT BODIES

★ Trailer Canteens, also built ★

WRITE OR CALL FOR PARTICULARS

GUARANTEED HEAT TREATED

A typical illustration of one of our bodies built on old or new chassis

HENDERSON'S
JOINERS AND COACHBUILDERS   Tel. 4335
Parr Street Saw Mills, St. Helens, Lancs.

The position continued for quite a while after the war, but relaxations were in sight and on 16th May 1949 the Ministry of Supply wrote to the Ministry of Transport suggesting that:-
'the impositions placed upon the commercial builders of motor vehicles and oil-fuelled goods vehicles might be eased, and the manufacturers of these items left to regulate supplies according to commercial demands.' This was an odd statement issued by a Government who had just nationalised the entire transport industry, but it may well be that it was the reaction to the political backlash that emerged to nationalisation. It is obvious that many small businesses were demanding access to their own forms of transport, and these relaxations may have been applied to appease this situation. The relaxation came into force on Monday 7th November 1949, and it is significant that many specialist bodybuilders began to expand their activities in the months that followed.

Before this date the bulk of the post-war bodybuilder's business had been re-bodying ex-military vehicles, including a significant number of American vehicles such as Chevrolet, Ford and so on. Times were changing however, and as the Austerity measures and rationing of the postwar period began to be less restrictive, affluence began to grow. Fruit and sweets were no longer luxuries, and ice cream also enjoyed a growing demand. To reflect this demand the Walls and Lyons Maid factories all took on more employees, whilst the Mayor of Nottingham opened a new works for the Pearce Ice Co. in April 1949. However, there was still no universal standard for the product and commenting on the problem Liverpool's City Analyst wrote 'No standards of composition have been fixed, so that ice cream may be anything from a frozen starch paste to a valuable food product, containing 10 per cent or more of fat, and the price charged bears no relation to the food value.' He continued 'Much controversy has occurred about this product, chiefly because ice cream includes any article sufficiently similar to ice cream as to constitute a substitute. This implies that practically anything white and frozen can be sold as ice cream.' That there were some dubious characters around can not be questioned, but the majority of makers were producing a wholesome fare, and even the bad ones had not resorted to the ancient tradition of snail slime!

That the business was expanding at a fantastic pace, we might show by the situation at the Pearce factory, where they were then producing many thousands of gallons of ice cream each week, whereas it had been just 50 gallons a week before war broke out ten years earlier. The increase in demand was staggering, and vending opportunities sprang up, especially during the summers of 1946 to 1948, the first years in which many had been able to take a seaside holiday since 1939. As a result the demand for mobile shops, sales kiosks etc. began to boom, and the May issue of *Commercial Motor* showed the ultimate in ice cream mobiling. This was in the form of 17' 6" (5.35m) long 2-wheeled trailer for Morcream Products by Wilsdons of Solihull. It had a perspex roof, fluorescent lights, a Bacterol steriliser, and its refrigerators, heating and cooking equipment could be powered by either calor gas or mains electric.

Above: *This wonderful, stylish mobile with a large expanse of glass is a Morrison-Electricar product from 1949, produced for Massarella & Sons in Leicester. It was an all-electric van on the SATH11 chassis and powered by Exide IM13D batteries. Its cost was £472.10s (£8,887).* ICA

Right: *This pre-war commercial is of unknown parentage, it may be a Morris, but the wire wheels, left-hand drive and offset radiator create quite a puzzle. Whatever, the chassis was re-bodied for Bennett's in 1951.*

Top Left: *This Alvis TA14 is representative of the type of large car chassis fitted with a custom coach-built body in the postwar era.*

Centre Left: *An advert for Brush Electric 10/14cwt, 18/22cwt and 25/cwt vehicles from 1944.*

Bottom Left: *A pair of Austin A70 10cwt vans based on the 2199cc Austin Hereford saloon a model that was built between 1950 and 1954.*

Above: *Not hugely dissimilar to the Morrison-Electricar model shown overleaf, the Morris J also carries a light, airy body with good visibility. Built by Cummins of Crewe this mobile was typical of the type being built on this chassis in 1953. The Morris J was a lively versatile 10/12cwt van, and it was used in a large number of service and utility fleets. The police, Royal Mail, Post Office Telephones and Gas Boards were amongst its devotees, and it was also used widely in ice cream vending. ICA*

Left: *Not all ice cream vendors were in a position to change to van-based mobiles, and the trike-handcart manufacturers managed to fight a reargaurd action. Many, like Pashley's looked at a cheaper form of propulsion, using motorcycles and mopeds as the basis. The MCT51 Superior's hinged front portion gave access to the gas burner, sterilising bowl, wash hand basin and other equipment. Pashleys are one firm that have survived the test of time, and are still with us today producing a range of quality products.*

Right: *Another Cummins-body is seen on a Fordson E83W chassis on the Newcastle Road, Shavington, near Crewe. The Cummins factory was located on this road behind the Eric Brookes Filling Station, and as a result it features in many of the early 'works' photographs. The 'factory' was initially based in a small part of what had been the service garage for Brookes but it later expanded and occupied about 3,000 sq. ft. Note the glass globes on the petrol and air pumps, the corrugated iron roof, and the Esso signs of the period. Alongside is a contemporary Cummins vehicle advert for 1952.*

By the early 1950s several new firms specialising in this type of business began to appear, among these was the firm of S. C. Cummins from Crewe who began building Mobile Shops and Ice Cream Mobiles in 1950. Cummins, along with a few others saw that speciality in this growing market could provide, if not a niche, then a nice little form of regular earning and they started advertising in the specialist ice cream press.

Amongst these early adverts Cummins are joined by Henderson's Joiners & Coachbuilders from St. Helens, Lancashire. Bryan Whitby, then with Cummins, recalls that the bulk of new chassis that were being bodied were the Austin/Morris J type and the Fordson E83W, although almost any chassis might have been used according to availability and customer preference. Cummins adverts featured the 'Wonderbar' (did a certain lingerie firm copy the name?) and the Morris 10cwt chassis, with body prices ranging from £90 (£1,500) to £300 (£5,000)! In Leeds, Appleyards were building quite large mobile cafes and ice cream parlours using wartime 'utility' bus chassis. Re-bodying old car chassis continued, and we know of at least one Rolls Royce (20 model) that was turned out as an ice cream mobile. A lot of pre-war Ford 10s and post-war Ford Pilots were purchased as saloon cars, and then cut down to chassis and bonnet, before rebuilding into mobiles. The Trojan was another model used in conversion, as were vans from the Bradford-based firm of Jowetts.

Electric vehicles (designed as milk floats) were seen as the ideal basis for ice cream delivery work, after all (within the urban areas) they were doing exactly the same work as the milk float, only at the opposite end of the day. Brush Electrical, Smiths, Morrison-Electricar and a few others promoted their models. Unfortunately, with the cost of the associated battery charging equipment it was not an economical option for the mobiler who only operated one or two vehicles as it worked out at around £1,250 (£20,500). Operating costs were very low however, so many mobilers struggled on with electric vehicles and in 1960 second-hand units were still fetching around £200 (£3,200). Morrison-Electricar seem to have built around 20, of which half were used in the South Wales area. Whether these were sent on trial or purchased is not known. A prototype of one of these vehicles is shown on page 19.

In 1945-6 Brush actually looked at producing a new flat bed battery-powered milk float for the United Dairies, on to which a demountable ice cream body could have been fitted. This would have meant that after milk delivery work was finished, the same vehicle could have done another 8-hour shift selling ice cream into the evening, and still had sufficient time for its batteries to be charged overnight. Quite why it never took off is not known, but had the big dairies got hold of this concept the small independent ice cream retailer would certainly have faced an uphill struggle.

WONDERBAR
MOBILE ICE CREAM SHOP
AND SNACKBAR ETC.
COMPLETELY FITTED INCLUDES
SINK AND HOT WATER GEYSER
ICE CREAM CONSERVATORS
Built on a Morris
10 cwt. Chassis. 12 h.p.
Trailer and Van Bodies
PRICES FROM £90 TO £300
WRITE FOR DETAILS
CUMMINS COACHBUILDERS
NEWCASTLE ROAD
SHAVINGTON, CREWE
TEL.: WYBUNBURY 296

Left: *A Morris J at the Cummins works at Shavington, seen prior to delivery to Tominey's City Ices. To the right will be seen the chassis of another J type and a Bedford CA, which is bound for Monikie in Angus, Scotland.*

Below: *A real Whitby Ice Cream Van, however this J Type has nothing to do with the firm of that name today, but is actually bound for the Yorkshire seaside resort of Whitby where it will work for Trillo Bros. Of interest are the three new Bedford CA chassis awaiting bodying at the Cummins works. Note that they only had a cowl and windscreen, and the delivery drivers just had crude wooden seats to bring the vehicles all the way from Luton.*

Top Right: *A completed CA pictured on the Newcastle road just before its despatch to Collettas of Willow Walk, London N5.*

Bottom Right: *A line up of at least five Bedford CAs in service with Jobes of Seaham, plus three other mobiles, possibly J Types.*

The advent of the Bedford CA chassis in 1952 was a major breakthrough, and whilst models like the Austin-Morris J, Fordson E83W, Commer-Karrier and even Standard Atlas became popular, the CA was soon the industry standard. By the late 1950s all the major builders were offering a CA body conversion. The Soft Ice Machine Company of London W1 offered a 'fully equipped ice cream van for less than £1,600' in other words a mere £26,000 at today's prices. Smiths offered two body versions, the Cornette Mk1 and MkII, promising £40 (£650) off to each new customer - mind you their advert does not say how much it cost in the first place.

The Picador Coachworks & Caravan Co. of Sholing, Southampton were another who used the CA in what they described as a 'Versatile and specially-designed van'. Up in Scotland, another of the industry leaders, Archibald Scott of Bellshill, Lanarkshire, were building, 'To The Highest Standards of Scottish Craftsmanship', the Ascol Minor Mobile Canteen using the 15cwt Bedford CASZ chassis, ash framing aluminium panels, fibreglass roof and formica interiors. What is more they offered immediate delivery as well, with the vans painted in two colours and lettered to the customers' requirements.

Top Left: *The Bedford CA was a medium range commercial van introduced in 1952 with a semi-forward control layout. It had a 1294cc engine, a 10/12cwt capacity and easy access sliding cab doors (although these doors did not feature on ice cream vans). This example was supplied to the firm of Dinky's of Belle Vue Station, Annan Road, Dumfries with a Cummins body in 1954.*

Bottom Left: *A later, long chassis version of the Bedford CA, this time with a 15cwt specification and first registered in 1961.*

Right: *A line up of newly built mobiles near the Morrison factory in Botley Road, Southampton in 1979. It features (from left to right) a Bedford CF, a Transit MkII and two more CFs. All four vehicles are HDV (hinge door vans) cut down panel vans with half bodies, whilst the fifth vehicle in the line up (another CF) was a chassis cowl carrying a full glass fibre body.*

The CA chassis, and all its contemporaries were, of course, still selling 'hard ice cream' and most were limited by the type of cabinets in which the sales items could be stored. The insulation and cooling, although effective, was limited in its versatility and soon the whole process of ice cream vending would change. This would come with the portable generator, which is also associated with the soft-ice revolution that will be discussed later.

In the pages that follow, kindly sponsored by Whitby Morrison, we give a potted history of ice cream mobiles in full glorious colour as no book on the subject would be complete without such illustrations. It is by no means comprehensive as many of the early vehicles were not photographed in colour, and those pictures that were taken tend to be of very poor quality. Added to this the demise of nearly all the major builders in recent years has seen the loss of valuable records and photographs etc.

Only Whitby Engineering remains, but their acquisition of Morrison (in 1988) and Cummins (in 1998) has enabled some of the records from these companies to be rescued. Undoubtedly other records are out there somewhere, and both authors wish to return to the subject in a later edition detailing all the body builders and chassis makers. We therefore accept that the section that follows is a little more modern than either of us would have liked, but we appeal to our readers to help rectify this situation in a future volume.

The Colourful World of Ice Cream Mobiles

CREAMY ALONZE'S ICES

AWARDS
DIPLOMAS
OF
MERIT
1954·68

Above: *An early Bedford CA with an unknown body owned by Alonze's ices, but typical of the type used in mobiling in the 1950s.*

Left: *This features another view of the preserved van shown on page 16, but in colour it presents a completely different aspect of this attractive ice cream mobile.*

A *Wall's* Bedford CA with Cummins Mk11 Bodywork

Above: *A Bedford CF featuring Cummins Mk17 bodywork for Walls Ice Cream, the body style ran from 1977 to 1982. Note the changes in colour scheme from the CA featured on page 27*

Left: *Another CF this time with a Cummins Mk12 body from the early 1970s.*

Right: *A MkI Transit, with a York diesel engine and a Cummins Mk13 body which was produced in the mid-1970s for a customer in the Mediterranean.*

Below: *MkII Transit with a body by Archibald Scott of Bellshill, for Marchetti Bros.* Ford of Great Britain.

Left: *This unusual Morris Mini features a low height body, and thus does not allow headroom for the operator to stand inside. It is seen here selling Lyons Maid products on the Rock of Gibraltar.*

Below: *Another British Leyland product sold to the foreign market was this late model Leyland FG, which was produced for NG enterprises in Hong Kong and the last one built on this chassis.*

Above: *In 1982 Bedford introduced the CF Mk2, and this picture shows a Cummins Mk21 body, and is seen in the Mr. Softee livery of the time.*

Right: *Another CF2, but this time one that was built as a demonstrator for Whitby's in 1984. After its promotional work it was sold to Mr. Marucci in Blackpool.*

Left: *The Leyland Sherpa was not the most popular of models in ice cream vending (as its engine was not then ideal for the direct drive system), and coupled with this unusual body style by Cummins it makes this a rare picture.*

Bottom Left: *The Sherpa's successor, the LDV series vans, were also not widely used in mobiling, although at the present time, negotiations are underway to explore possibilities of future development with LDV. So this fleet of four Cummins mobiles on the 400 series chassis for Saudi Arabia is also very unusual, although similar mobiles were exported as far away as New Zealand.*

Right: *Here we see a Renault Traffic which utilised the original factory-built high roof, although this necessitated additional strengthening and lining. Cummins exported quite a few of these to Holland, and the one pictured here went to Northern Ireland. However, the Renault Traffic was not a widely adopted chassis for this type of work.*

Below: *This Mercedes 307 chassis is fitted with a Whitby body, and built for Colin Deakin of Doncaster who operates a Mr. Softee franchise. Interestingly, the registration plate comes from an earlier Mr. Softee van with a Smiths body on a Commer chassis.*

A New Era

This is one of the first true Whitby-Morrison vehicles built in Crewe, which appeared in 1990 following the acquisition of Morrison the year before. The Morrison business had suffered in the troubled financial years of the early-1980s, and it was eventually bought out by Robin Hood Vehicle Builders in 1983, but ice cream vehicles only formed a very small part of their operation. When Robin Hood looked at the market, they decided that this did not form part of their future strategy, and they approached Whitby Engineering to see if they were interested in continuing the operation. The well-known Morrison body moulding was then developed by Whitby's, who retained many of the best features but modified them to meet the needs of the 1990s (and beyond).

Right: *This is undoubtedly the best Cummins body ever produced in Crewe. Fitted to the Mercedes Sprinter chassis, it forms the pinnacle of Cummins production. However, it was one of the last to be built at the Quaker's Coppice Works, before the Cummins range was acquired by Whitby Engineering in 1998. Since then this style has been further refined by Whitby, and remains in production today.*

Below: *An example of a Cummins Mk17 body adapted to suit the Chevrolet van chassis, and supplied to Saudi Arabia in the early 1980s. As the century draws to its end, David Cummins is working with Stuart Whitby to develop a market for traditional British ice cream mobiles in America and at the time of writing the first Chevrolet chassis has arrived at Crewe for bodying.*

Overleaf: *Three pictures that really demonstrate the colourful world of ice cream. Obviously the product speaks for itself, but the other two illustrations show the sign-writers art. The two transits are both products of the Whitby factory, the upper one is a Whitby long cowl van, whilst the bottom one has a Cummins Mk23 body. Their colourful scenes were hand painted by the firm's two artists Alan Claire and Terry Wallker.*

35

The Soft Ice Cream Revolution

The story that follows is quite fascinating, for what happened next (as our title implies) was quite a revolution for the industry. For the change from traditional (hard) ice cream to soft ice cream influenced the way that the mobile vending market would thereafter develop. The 10 to 15cwt chassis range was still widely used for hard ice cream, but many were also used on soft ice cream work. Most of the mid-range light commercials thus employed were usually fitted with Onan electricity generating sets. Other types of generators were tried but most were either noisy in operation or less than reliable.

The small generators had an output of 5kva, and could power equipment up to 3hp, but at around 350-400lbs (158-181kg) they must have been constantly near the maximum weight limits for the 10-15cwt chassis. More powerful 7.5Kva generators were available, and the most common were the Workman-Reed TVO/Petrol 'Beacon' power units, but Ford 100E and small BMC engines (such as the Austin A35 and Morris 1000) were also quite widely used.

Above: *The advent of soft-ice mobiles saw an increasing growth in chassis size to cope with all the added weight of the generating equipment used on the soft-ice machine. This Commer 1-ton van was supplied to an independent retailer in Buxton, Derbyshire.*

All these larger units added considerable weight, and the mid-range light commercials were simply not up to the job. The alternatives were the 30cwt BMC LD chassis, and the Commer-Karrier 1-ton/1.25-ton chassis. Of course it is with the later chassis that the soft-ice cream machine is best known. So popular was this Routes Group product, that by the end of 1961 nearly 2,000 had been sold for ice cream vending. Most of the leading firms were bodying the Commer-Karrier chassis, as we will discuss later. It was also the chassis on which the innovative Mr. Whippy and Mr. Softee mobiles had set the trend in the 1959 season. It was soon copied by other firms who were looking at the 'brand image' and franchise concept. With the success of the combines, it was not long before the small independent operators began to enter the soft-ice cream market using their mobiles as ice cream factories on wheels.

The soft-ice cream concept had been brought to Britain by Dominic Facchino whose family had done much to protect the small ice cream vendor after World War I, when they began producing the Facchino powder mix. They also set up the Facchino biscuit company, but in 1956 the family firm was sold out to the Neilson Company of Canada who had begun making ice cream in Toronto in 1893. The founder of Neilson's himself having been inspired by Thomas Webb. With the takeover Facchino went to Neilsons, but he still wanted to run his own business. Shortly after the takeover Facchino was in America, where he saw an ice cream van which he later described as 'A little ice cream factory on wheels!'

What he saw was probably one of the trucks operated by brothers William and James Conway of Philadelphia, who had begun their soft-ice business on St. Patrick's Day 1956. The very first soft-ices were in fact given away that day, and appropriate to the occasion they were coloured green. The Conways went on to become Mister Softee, but their concept impressed Facchino so much that he came back to Britain and gave up his £5,000 (£60,000) per year job. In 1958 with a capital of £100 (£1,200) he started his new firm. There were four of them at the time, Facchino, his two sisters and his old colleague, Peter Hopkins. It was hard work at the start, but with soft ice cream vans taking around £300 (£3,600) per week or around three times as much as a hard ice cream van, the business boomed.

Top Left: *These early two machines based in a Walls Austin LD are the Carpigiani 'Singola' soft ice cream machines, which were specifically produced for mobile operation. This picture is very unusual, as it was not common for two single machines to be put in one van, and where higher output was required the 'Doppia' double machine would be used. The 'Doppia' allowed the sale of two flavours, as for example strawberry and vanilla, and this picture suggests that this arrangement may have pre-dated the Doppia.*

Bottom Left: *By the late 1950s the advent of better hygiene standards meant an improvement in the internal specifications of the mobiles, and this picture in a Walls van shows why. For a start we have a fully lined interior, with the use of Formica laminates, giving wipe clean surfaces. Hot and cold water, for hand washing, was also introduced. Continual improvement and regulation has ensured that modern vehicles meet all the required standards. Stainless-steel refrigerators, moulded interiors and one-piece anti-slip floor coverings are all part of the modern mobile*

Right: *In the back of this BMC Walls 'Super Whip' van, sits a 12.5kva generator connected to a proprietary motor vehicle engine. It would initially be started on petrol, and after ten minutes warm up, would be changed over to TVO operation using a cheaper 'paraffin-based' fuel known as tractor vapourising oil. It was a common fuel of the period, but already tractor manufacturers had begun to move rapidly away from TVO to diesel or petrol engines.*
All images courtesy Birds-Eye Walls

In an article in *Ice Cream & Frozen Confectionery* of September 1958, it states that the first British mobile ice cream factory had been built by Smiths of Gateshead for the Mr. Softee organisation of the United States. Quite who can claim to be the first firm in Britain is open to debate, but they were probably both contemporary with one another. It is quite appropriate to say that, as far as mobile sales went, the public really did prefer the soft ices to the hard ice creams that had previously been the only choice.

In 1961 the *Daily Telegraph* said 'the new soft ice cream seller has emulated the quality of ice creams sold in dairy parlours, but he brings it right to your door at no extra cost.' Inside three years the two 'Mister' businesses went from strength to strength, and many others copied it. In an interview in 1962 Facchino said, 'I estimated that I needed to gain a two-year lead over the big firms, otherwise they could blot me out. It was a big gamble.'

It may have been a gamble but it paid off, and in 1960 Mr. Whippy recorded profits of £50,000 (£600,000), the next year it had shot up to £200,000 (£2.4 million). In 1962 Facchino sold the business to Charles Forte in return for shares in the Forte Empire worth £1 million (£12 million). By then the company had 900 vehicles (mostly built by Morrison Electrofreeze in Southampton) and 1,000 employees. They also had a new factory at Basildon making 3 million gallons of ice cream mix each year, and a network of 26 depots around the country. Facchino remained as Chairman of the Whippy organisation, and he presided over its continued expansion. In 1963 they moved into the petrol filling station business, although most were bought for depots to house the vans overnight. Sales kiosks were opened at Motorway service stations, and the Whippy vans went on to the continent, whilst the new cone factory at Tamworth turned out 20,000,000 cones every month.

The sheer volume of it all scared the big firms to death, and they too entered the soft-ice business, but Whippy had the edge. Facchino attributed his success to hard work and a willingness to reward employee loyalty with a share of the profits. However Charles Forte's biography shows a different light, for he states:-

'Our accountants studied the figures and recommended the purchase. I was also impressed by the chairman and managing director of the company. But I had made a mistake. As soon as I bought the company, the management seemed to lose all interest and it was not long before Mr. Whippy was losing a lot of money. I decided to cut the losses and we sold out to Walls, who were no doubt glad to eliminate a competitor whilst increasing the size of their own operation. The losses on this deal were over £500,000 (£6 million): it was a complete failure and in many ways a salutary experience. It proved to us that we were by no means infallible. It also taught me a lesson - never acquire a business however good it may appear to be, unless you are either guaranteed continuity of management or you are in a place to replace the management.'

Above: *This superb (but un-dated) view of the Walls repair workshops gives a good idea of the scale of the company's road vehicle operation. Here we see at least seven Commer-Karrier 1-ton vans in for repair or service, along with at least two fibreglass Morrison-bodied Bedford CAs and two 8-wheel AEC bulk delivery lorries. In the background, the use of a magnifying glass shows that a Ford 307E and a Morris J2 van are also in the depot but in an obviously disused state.* Birds-Eye Walls

The popularity of the soft ice cream van forced many independent traders to look at this threat to their business, and by the Spring of 1960 the makers were advertising soft serve vehicles with the benefits of independence, no ties, and the ability to use one's own mix. For example Cummins were advertising 'Mobile Ice Cream Factories' for £2,400 (£29,000). Based on the Austin 30cwt chassis it came complete with Sweden Freezer, generator, 2-temperature conservator, and hot & cold water. A similar priced van was produced by Cream Line Soft Serve Vehicles of Birmingham.

It is interesting to compare the cost of these vans with the Jaguar E type which was shortly to be launched at a price of £2,100 (£25,250). Conversely the price of the traditional hard ice van dropped appreciably, for example the firm of Vincent Greenhous in Wrexham were offering a Bedford CA in primer for £675 (£8,100). Stoker Bros from Stoke-on-Trent, who won first prize at the Ice Cream Alliance Show in Southport in 1960, were selling their CA fully lettered at £800 (£9,600). The CA was putting up a fight, but it was clearly losing, Ford (with their 10-15cwt Thames 400E) were making some progress, but the Super Beacon TVO/Petrol 7.5KVA generator made them 'back-end heavy' and as the standard Thames van could be a little skittish at times, several 'incidents' occurred.

The Onan generator, whilst lighter, did not have the performance of the larger types so talk of heavier vehicles became the norm. Smiths of Gateshead for example were offering the 2-ton Commer-Karrier 'Walk-Thru' with a mid-mounted generator. The same firm were still very busy with the 1-ton Karrier Cruiser, which they were producing in large quantities for the Mr. Softee organisation. Electrofreeze (who became a division of A C Morrison) were also taking large quantities of the Commer-Karrier, the majority of which were bodied for the Mr. Whippy organisation. Bonallack and Cummins were building on both the BMC and Commer-Karrier chassis. The Motor Delivery Company of Northallerton were, with Mr. Really Good, promoting their Economica Van (based on the BMC 30cwt chassis with a Super Beacon generator) as having a 6 shilling (£3.60) a day operating cost.

At the other end of the scale IPAX of London W1 offered the 3-wheeled Crescent Carrier (based around a small moped) for £310 (£3,700). What was advertised as 'a truly magnificent mobile' was subject to road tax at £6 (£72) per annum, and achieved 100mpg with its fan-cooled engine. Lambretta, Vespa and BSA scooters and motorcycles were also being built with cabinets for hard ice cream sales, as a cheaper alternative to the new soft ice vendors.

Top Right: *This Bedford CA in the Walls Fleet shows how the Onan 4CCK-57RV generator was fitted in a Smith-built body. It produced 5kw, weighed 375lbs and would power a fridge and a single soft-ice machine, but the Onan adverts claimed it would power a twin head machine? Negligible soundproofing and heavy rear-end weight are obvious disadvantages. Birds-Eye Walls.*

Bottom Right: *This picture is fairly typical of one of the new 'independent' soft ice cream vans that began to appear in 1961. The franchise concept had already deterred many, and some were warning mobilers not to sign up to such agreements without careful consideration. Yet the public wanted soft ice, so the independents went to the makers for soft ice vans and they duly began to oblige. Smiths and Morrison were busy with the Mr. Softee and Mr. Whippy organisations, but firms like Cummins were able to oblige. This BMC LD was sold to a Mr. Morris, ironically the badge adhered to the front proclaims it to be an Austin, not a Morris!*

The Industry Giants

Above: *With a 1959 tax disc this CA carries the Eldorado logo (with its walking polar bear), and worked in Staffordshire.*

The advent of the soft-ice revolution severely impacted on the existing companies, and it is clear that 'branding' and associated advertising were to play an important role. Walls and Lyons Maid were major players, but a few other names should be recalled for the sake of completeness. We have already mentioned Mr. Whippy and Mr. Softee, but there was another attempt at a franchise operation by 'Mr. Really Good'. The promoters of this brand were Rea's Creamy Ices of Folkestone who were well-known for their manufacture of processed liquid mix and frozen confections. This organisation initially approached their local body builders Martin Walter, but they were heavily committed to Bedford CA conversion work. Walters were reluctant to fit the 7.5kv diesel generating set to the 15-17cwt chassis, as a result Rea's chose the BMC 30cwt chassis, and had it bodied by the Motor Delivery Co in distant Northallerton.

Eldorado was another of the 'brands' that developed in the 1950s, and it was on sale in several cinemas, and in many of the high street shops like those belonging to the F. W. Woolworth chain. The precise details of mobiling operations are not all that clear, and a search of the various trade journals has not been all that helpful. In view of the authors' desire to cover the subject in much greater detail in a future book, we would again appeal to our readers for information. As far as the vehicles employed in the Eldorado operation, it seems as though the bulk were based on the Bedford CA chassis, although at least one was built around the Ford Thames 400E. That Eldorado were a major player in the industry for a while can be recognised, but they were acquired by Lyons Maid in 1963, which saw the subsequent closure of Eldorado's London factory soon after, and the gradual assimilation of the Eldorado brand into Lyons Maid.

The Neilson company has already been mentioned with regard to the early ice cream development in Canada, and this firm (owned by multi-millionaire Garfield Weston) took over the Facchino business in Britain in 1956. They developed a franchise operation, and offered 'exclusive' territories and easy finance on Bedford CA mobiles and, as the advert (right) shows, they later mounted a campaign to sell an easy scoop ice to combat the soft-ice revolution after Dominic Facchino set up Mr. Whippy. They later adopted the name Lord Neilson and merged with Lyons Maid in 1962, with complete absorption in 1966. Another venture was the Tonibell operation, which was started by Tony Peters in the early 1950s, and used Harvin musical chimes to attract the customers. The technique was highly successful, and in turn it attracted the attention of the British American Tobacco Co., and was acquired by them in 1964.

Below: *This Tonibell Bedford CAL (with its roof-mounted cow) was photographed for the* Daily Mirror *in November 1969, when the company changed the livery from blue to 'Hunting Pink'. The new colour was so vivid it was known in the trade as kinky pink.*

Ice cream from sausages might sound a little far-fetched, but that is how the British ice cream industry leaders of today started their life. It is a fascinating history which, like the Barham and Lyons story, goes back to the early part of the industrial revolution as London began to develop. We start in 1786 with a butcher called Edmund Cotterill, who opened a shop in St. James's Market to make sausages. His business thrived, and with Londoners liking his sausages, he very soon decided to take on an apprentice called Richard Wall. In 1807 the business passed from Cotterill to Wall, and it continued to thrive, so much so that in 1812 it gained a Royal Appointment to make sausages for King George II. Walls products became very fashionable as a result and a new shop was acquired at 113, Jermyn Street in the West End of London in 1834.

Shortly after this move Wall must have died, because the firm was renamed Ann Wall & Son. The son was the first Thomas Wall, and he took over the running of the business in 1840. Thomas had two sons follow him into the business Thomas II, and Frederick and by 1870 they were running the operation. They only sold quality pork products, but they never varied their price, no matter what the price of pork may be. Royal patronage continued and it is reported that Queen Victoria would have special hampers prepared by the Wall's family for whenever she was travelling away from London.

In 1903 the Wall's family opened a purpose-built factory at Battersea Park, and a delivery operation was commenced using ten new horsedrawn vans. Six were based at Battersea, the rest worked from Jermyn Street. In 1905 the firm became a limited company, and an association was begun with another sausage-making firm, Davis & Hollis from Oxford Street (who had a factory in Acton). This firm was managed by a dynamic young man called Lionel Rodd, and he had a brother (Charles) who was a partner in a sausage-making business in Poole, Dorset. Thomas Wall II, a confirmed bachelor, was now advancing in years and he viewed the Rodd's as being the men to takeover from him. However, the merger did not go ahead until after World War I, but a condition of the deal saw the closure of the factories at Poole and Battersea, and the construction of a modern plant at the Friary in Acton which opened in 1920.

In 1919 Lord Leverhulme approached Frederick Wall, with a view to the firm becoming associated with his MacFisheries operation. In 1920 the association was cemented, and Walls became part of Lever Brothers. The two Rodd brothers and Mr. A.G. Short were appointed as joint managing directors. They continued to develop the Walls brand, but they also faced a major problem as the British public were reluctant to eat pork in the summer, and this meant that staff had to be either laid off or alternate work found.

The matter came up one day in 1913, when a discussion of the summer problem took place between Charles Rodd and Mr. Short, which was overheard by a clerk in the Poole factory. The clerk looked at his superiors and said, 'Why not do what the Americans do, and make ice cream'. This casual remark was to be the catalyst in the growth of Walls ice cream, although World War I was to intervene in the implementation of the idea. In 1922 Charles Rodd sent his son, Cecil, to Chicago in order to learn the ice cream business. On his return to England, he set to work in a factory that had been constructed at Acton in his absence. The new factory was capable of producing several thousand gallons a week, but the sales were very disappointing, as retailers were reluctant to stock the product. To overcome this Walls began their tricycle operation selling ice cream direct to the public. That the project was a success can be measured by the fact that the 10 cycles acquired in 1922, had grown to a fleet of 8,500 in 1939.

By the start of World War II Walls had 160 depots, and had opened a second ice cream factory in Manchester and a solid carbon dioxide 'dry ice' factory in Acton. The success was bound to continue, but early in World War II the Government prohibited the manufacture of ice cream, and the plant was turned over to the manufacture of margarine, powdered milk, dried eggs and canned orange juice. Large quantities of tinned meats, sausage, lard and dripping were also made. The resumption of peace saw an early return to ice cream manufacture, and by 1949 sales had climbed back to the pre-war levels. In the bad winter of 1947 it is recorded that, when the delivery vans could not get through to North Devon, the deliverymen took their supplies through by sledge. The success of Walls Ice Cream has been phenomenal, and a major step was the acquisition of Mr. Whippy in 1966. Today Walls are one of the major world producers, and this really forms quite another story!

Top Left: *This late-1940s Walls mobile shop is built on an Austin FX3 chassis. This was not a common chassis for ice cream work and it was more commonly associated with taxi work - large numbers of the FX3 formed the basis for London's fleet of black cabs.* Birds Eye-Walls

Top Right: *This Morris J type was No.1036 in the fleet of T. Walls Ltd., The Friary, Acton, London W3. It is fairly typical of the vending vehicles employed by the company in that period. The price list displayed internally shows that cones and brickettes were 3 old pence, whilst tubs and choc-ices were 5 old pence.*

Centre Right: *Seen new in 1959, No.2778 was a Morrison-Electricar battery-electric mobile. Developed from their milk float chassis, this was a brave attempt to produce an economical, versatile vehicle for local delivery fleet work. For the independent trader, the ancillary battery charging equipment usually meant that the price was prohibitive.*

Bottom Right: *The standard Walls van for many years was based on a 30cwt Morris commercial chassis. This LD version, No.2618, dates from 1959, but does not carry the standard Walls body of the time.*

As we mentioned earlier, Joseph Lyons began trading with a small chain of tobacconist shops and went on to become a world leader in the food industry. Indeed, there will be few readers who have not tried Lyons coffee or a Lyons cake, and many will fondly remember that quite British institution, the Lyons Corner House. This chain of cafes reached its pinnacle between the two world wars, and as the years went by, the name became synonymous with quality at an affordable price. Their distinctive blue and white vans were to be seen all over Britain, delivering all manner of foodstuffs.

In the mid-1920s, the company decided to expand its operations into ice cream wholesaling, but the product it had sold for years in the Corner Houses soon began to appear in small shops and cafes up and down the country. A fleet of dark blue and cream vans were employed for the distribution work, but I have not been able to determine exactly when the company began direct mobile sales. The first advertisements and news items appear in the latter part of 1944, so it may well be that they were gearing up for the sales that were bound to come with the resumption of peace. In 1947 they bought out Walkers Dairies from Liverpool and in 1951 went on to acquire Glacier foods (a manufacturer of ice lollies) from Maidenhead.

In October 1946, Lyons placed an order with the Trojan company of Croydon for 50 of their new 1-ton chassis, fitted with Perkins diesel engines. The order states that they were required for mobile sales of dairy products (was this a novel way of getting round the restriction of building ice cream vans?), however there is no record of who would carry out the bodywork. This seems to have been the start of their mobiling operation, which was then boosted when Massarellas Supplies of Dorchester were bought out in 1954.

Lyons maintained their brand image for around 12 more years, but as a consequence of the changes in the industry, they decided to make some radical changes in 1957. After opening a new factory at Bridge Park, Middlesex, Lyons introduced a new brand name as a major stroke of policy to push sales even higher. A statement was circulated to all retail outlets and an advertising film was distributed to cinemas (such was the power of this advertising medium at that time), and the name of Lyons Maid was born for the 1957 summer season. The heatwave of 1959 was a boom time, but the advent of soft ice cream onto the British market that year was to impact heavily on the traditional manufacturers like Lyons Maid and Walls, and by 1960 their sales had begun to show a marked decline.

The soft scoop ices of the Neilson operation were one solution, and by combining the Lyons Maid and Neilson operations in 1962 bigger and better mobile shop sales were achieved. In 1965 the well-known ice cream business of Bertorelli was purchased, but the outright acquisition of Mr. Softee and the purchase of Midland Counties Dairy (in 1970) were significant. Another was the Tonibell operation, which had grown from humble beginnings to a net worth of £1.75 million when Lyons bought it from the giant conglomerate British American Tobacco Ltd. in 1969.

By this time Lyons had grown into a major business empire, owning shops hotels, restaurants and even the Wimpy hamburger chain. We can not cover the diversity of all the Lyons' operations, but we can mention that the company was split into various 'groups'. The Lyons Maid brand was now part of Glacier Foods Ltd., which was a holding company that controlled several well-known ice cream operations. Glacier was owned by Lyons, Union International and Nestle, all of which were closely associated with ice cream manufacture or vending. At the height of operations Lyons Maid were centred on four factories and a network of around 70 depots. Their vans were mostly Bedford CAs, but a number of Ford Thames 400E chassis were fitted with soft-ice machines in 1960. A light van policy was also adopted, with Minis, Ford 307E, the Bedford/Vauxhall HA chassis, Marinas and Escorts all being used.

Glacier then developed its three franchising operations, Mr. Softee, Tonibell and Lyons Maid. Support for the franchisees was very strong, and at head office a 16-strong team were on hand to deal with mobiling issues, complemented by nine area managers out in the field. The 1970s saw a great deal of change but this time it was caused by 'the oil crisis', which resulted in inflation and operating costs moving ahead of profitability. Franchising became less successful as rising costs forced operators to buy cheaper products, in turn the level of support given was reduced. As a consequence the number and quality of the vehicles reduced dramatically, and by the mid-1980s the franchise operation was all but finished. In 1992 Nestle purchased the Lyons Maid brand, and a major review of the position was instituted. In 1998 Nestle relaunched its mobiling sector, and an exciting new era had begun!

Top Left: *Based on Ford's popular 100E saloon, this 5cwt van version was known as the 300E Ford Thames. Used mainly for delivery work with insulated rear compartments, J. Lyons & Co. purchased over 300 of these vehicles direct from Dagenham.*

Top Right: *This Trojan 570 HMV has survived its brethren from the Lyons Maid fleet, and has now become a preserved vehicle.*

Centre Right: *By using smaller vehicles with lower capital costs and cheaper running costs, Lyons Maid were able to keep a leading edge in the market until they acquired the Mr. Softee operation.*

Bottom Right: *After the Nestle's acquisition of the Lyons Maid brand, a new image began to appear. Today smart blue vans are prominent but there have been some interesting variations such as this Mercedes Sprinter supplied to Midland Super Ice Cream.*

Mobile Shops & Kiosks

It has already been stated that the builders of mobiles had generally progressed from the 'build anything' attitude of the postwar coachbuilders to more specialist producers. Of course many general firms remained in operation, but the number of ice cream mobiles they produced was diminishing as the 'mobile specialists' grew in size and experience. However, it should not be forgotten that, for much of the time covered by this account, the bodybuilders who were constructing ice cream mobiles were also turning out other body types on fairly similar chassis.

After all, if you could build an attractive mobile shop to sell ice creams, the same basic concept could be employed for greengrocers, butchers, fishmongers, bakers and general grocers. Fish and chip vans, tea bars, hot-dog vans, mobile libraries, milk floats and even travelling banks were also within the remit of the builders. Smiths of Gateshead were among the market leaders, but Cummins, Picador, Bonallack, Martin Walter, Archibald Scott, Morrison, and a host of others were all selling into a market that seemed to have no boundaries. A decline would set in as the 'supermarket' concept grew, but in the 1950s the mobile shop was very popular indeed.

It was not just the supermarket, but also the mobility of the general public that led to the demise of the mobile shop, but these wonderful vehicles still have their strongholds. The area around the Trans-Pennine offices in rural Cumbria has two firms operating large fleets of mobile bread vans and general shops. Mobile libraries are still required, and even the travelling bank has not completely vanished, but the surviving builders tend to obtain most of their business from the food vending business.

The technology applied to ice cream mobiles was transferred to food vending very early in the specialist building era, and the sales literature of the builders nearly always shows a 'hot food' version of the ice cream van. For example the Cummins catalogues show that a Bedford CA 'Fish & Chip' van would cost £950 (£10,337) in 1962, by 1969 a BMC Mini 'Hot Dog' van was priced at £744 (£5,981), and three years later a Vauxhall Viva 'Chicken Barbecue' mobile sold for £1,040 (£8,361). Also in 1972 another builder, Pollocks of Motherwell, offered the BMC 250JU travelling shop starting at £1,350 (£10,854) and the Morris 1000 'American Hamburger' unit at £999 (£8,031). We could spend a considerable time discussing this type of business, but the subject of mobile shops and milk floats is so intriguing that the publishers intend to produce separate books on the subjects. Once again we would appeal for the assistance of the readership in identifying this particular part of the industry.

Before leaving the subject of the additional activities of the bodybuilders, we must mention the trailers and caravans used for mobiling. In their own right this subject would fill a substantial part of this book, but in the space available we can just briefly mention them. The trailer kiosk has always been an integral part of ice cream vending and in many ways one step on from the trike. The kiosks varied in size and function, and by way of example we can mention that in 1962 Ocean Trailers of Crewe advertised a 6ft x 4ft trailer for £225 (£2,448), whilst at the other end of the scale Picador of Southampton were offering an 18ft x 7ft twin wheel catering trailer for £695 (£7,561).

Top Left: *This mobile shop, built by Cummins on an Austin LD was supplied to the Shropshire firm of C&J Roche in Wellington. It sold; Bread, Confectionery, Fruit & Vegetables, Birthday Cakes, Frozen Foods and, believe it or not, even ice creams!*

Bottom Left: *This Ford Thames Trader carries a longer Cummins body and was used by Green Shield Stamps as a mobile redemption shop where trading/saving stamps could be exchanged for goods.*

Top Right: *A traditional Picador kiosk used by Walls.*

Centre Right: *A single wheel Cummins trailer fitted out as a snack bar for Andersons c1958 and very advanced for its day.*

Bottom Right: *A Cummins twin-wheel trailer of the mid-1990s, it carries a generator to power the soft ice cream machine.*

Ringing The Changes

Perhaps the most distinctive feature about ice cream mobiles for almost fifty years, has been the chimes or electrical bells that are used to herald the arrival of the vehicle at its vending point. Originally the ice cream man would announce his presence by the use of a large hand bell or, in the case of a trike, a cycle bell. However, with the advent of motorised vending, it was soon discovered that a more effective bell could be powered by the van's electrical system. In the early 1950s a number of specialist firms started up, and of these Harvins still produce chimes today. We asked Barry Older to say a few words about this development.

'In 1954 Ron Peters of Tonibell came to Harvin with a large American chime unit, which employed tuned metal bars struck by metal hammers to make a tune. He asked for a smaller, more reliable unit, so Bob Vincent and Raye Harris developed a system that consisted of a hand tuned Swiss musical movement (of a type found in music boxes), and fitted this with a magnetic pick-up. As this was before the days of transistors, the amplifiers used radio-type valves. Power was supplied from a 240v DC supply from an in-built generator. The system worked well but it used a lot of power and drained batteries were not uncommon.

Despite this foible the chimes were so successful in promoting sales that they became very popular indeed. In 1958 reliable transistors came on to the market, and efficient amplifiers were built to work directly from the vehicle's battery. They only used a small amount of power, and some of these early chimes are still in daily use today. Within a year the chimes had ceased to be a novelty, and all knew they were the best method of advertising the presence of an ice cream van. They have also been used on other kinds of food vending vehicles as well. Recent years have seen the introduction of electronic chimes with several tunes in one unit, but with a 'computerised' sort of sound. But the traditional musical movement is still the most readily recognised way to attract customers!'

Interestingly, the cost of the units is now less than they were years ago. For example a Standard unit from Harvins in 1969 would cost £39.15s (£320), whereas today a unit of the equivalent output like the Pied Piper set would cost £234.50. Twelve-volt fluorescent lights were another innovation, costing £5.6s (£53) in 1963, but available today for around £38. However, all this extra equipment presented the problem of additional weight on the already well-laden chassis. But two new innovations would solve this in the mid-1960s.

By the 1960s coachbuilt bodies were facing ever-increasing payloads and heavy fixed equipment, especially on vehicles like fire appliances, ambulances and ice cream vans. It was obvious that something would have to be done to reduce the weight, and a start was made with the introduction of fibreglass roofs being fitted to the ash-framed aluminium bodies by firms like Appleyard in Leeds. This was a short step away from complete fibreglass bodies, and in ice cream vending it seems as though this step was taken in 1961 when an almost complete fibre glass body by Moto Plastics was fitted to the BMC LD chassis by the Motor Delivery Co. In 1962 this firm offered a complete fibre glass body (seen page 5), but it was Morrison who really developed the concept in 1964/5.

The difficulty was still the enormous weight of the two types of generators that were being employed on the mobiles, and it was not until 1962 that the problem was solved by Bryan Whitby. He looked at the problem and thought that there must be a simpler, less-expensive means to power soft ice cream machines. At that time several companies were experimenting with all sorts of ideas and the nearest to success was a belt drive system powered by a Vellocette LE motorcycle engine. The result was not as reliable (or quiet) as the designers hoped for! Yet the concept inspired Bryan to employ the belt drive, although he questioned the need to carry a secondary power unit. As with most good ideas, Bryan's idea was simple, as he says 'I thought why not use the vehicle engine to power the ice cream machinery via drive belts from the crankshaft pulley and a shaft mounted electro magnetic clutch.'

This direct drive was set to radically change the production of ice cream in vehicles, and hence alter the market for the product. By eliminating the need for a generator and separate engine, it was then possible to feature soft ice cream equipment in the lighter and lower cost 15cwt chassis like the Bedford CA. In addition to the lower purchase price, the running costs were more economical, and thus the system was of great appeal. In January 1965 Bryan Whitby and S.C. Cummins filed a Patent application for Mobile Ice Cream Producing Equipment, which featured an 'engine-driven vehicle with a compressor for the ice cream refrigeration and a beater for soft-ice whipping, comprising shaft-driven electromagnetic clutches both energised by the battery, which was also charged by the driving mechanism.' The patent was issued as No.1,084,181 in September 1967. Today the Whitby system is the accepted standard, and is in use all over the world.

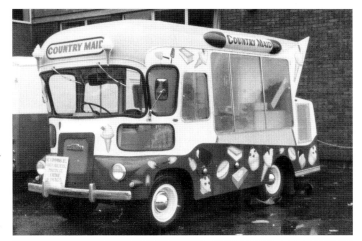

Top Left: *By the use of direct drive to power the soft-ice machines, vendors could return to the 15-17cwt chassis, where the Bedford CA (with a Whitby drive) became a clear favourite.*

Top Right: *A traditional heavy body on a Morris LD chassis.*

Centre Right: *The Cummins Conquest on the Austin LD chassis has the same problem, despite its 'futuristic' styling, but it was a Cummins engineer who was to solve the problem!*

Bottom Right: *This Bedford CA for Mr.Whippy is believed to have one of the first all-fibreglass bodies produced by Morrison-Electrofreeze.*

The Small Mobile Concept

The concept of using small vehicles was a direct result of the soft-ice phenomenon, as the sellers of hard ices needed to create a more effective means of selling. The answer seems to have been spawned by Walls and Eldorado who both began using small 5-7cwt vans for vending. The Walls Fords 307E, perhaps the best known of the small mobiles, were bodied by Martin Walter of Folkestone, and were really little 'kiosks' on wheels. The vans were left-hand drive, as it was intended that the driver/salesman would need to get out of his van and serve from the outside. As may be imagined, these were not popular with the salesmen, and the 307Es were soon sold off. Barry Glover, then at Walls, recalls that a number were sold onto the continent (France, Italy and so on) whilst others were rebodied by firms like Cummins and Morrison and turned into walk-thru vans.

But both Walls and Lyons Maid kept faith with small vans, and Morrison-Electrofreeze were bodying both the Bedford HA and Ford Thames vans for each company, but the vehicles were now provided with greater headroom so that the operator could serve from within. The vehicle production costs were much lower than the 30cwt or 1-ton chassis used for soft-ice vending, so with lower purchase prices and better running costs, the 'small van' salesman could fight his rearguard action against the new franchise operations. A variety of vehicles were used for this type of mobile, including the three models shown on this page. However, vehicles like the Austin A35, Austin A50, Morris 1000 and even the Hillman Husky were converted. In later years the Ford Escort, Morris Marina and Hillman Avenger were used.

The Bedford CA and CF models were still the most widely used vehicles in the hard-ice trade, but there were some distinct advantages to adopting the 5-7cwt chassis. We can demonstrate this by comparing the price of a Bedford CA with the alternative small vans. In 1962 Cummins offered the CA at £699.15s (£7,697), Picador were offering the Morris 1000 at £501.10s (£5,516). In 1969 Cummins offered the Bedford CA at £909 (£7,272) or the Bedford HA/Vauxhall Viva at £825 (£6,600), and the BMC Mini at £768 (£6,144). These prices compared favourably with the soft-ice vehicles where the CA was £1,780 (£14,240) and the BMC LD at £2,540 (£20,320).

Top Left: *BMC Mini vans were produced in the Austin and Morris guises, and were relatively successful vehicles despite their 'top heavy' appearance. They were also much narrower than their counterparts, so adjustments had to be made to the body moulding. A typical example is this 1965 Morris with a Cummins body.*

Centre Left: *This Walls Ford Thames 307E van was part of a large fleet; one has since been fully restored at the Whitby works.*

Bottom Left: *With a slightly similar body style to the Mini above, this HA van of 1966 carries the 'Batman' style Cummins body. Note the tail fins and bulbous eyes above the cab area.*

The Advent Of The Transit

We have already mentioned the Ford Thames 400E van which, although a very useful light commercial, was not widely adopted by the ice cream vending industry. The successor to the Thames was to be another story however. It began in 1961 when Ford appointed an American planner, Ed Baumgartner, to set up 'Redcap' a Common European Van project. He stayed with the project until it came to fruition late in 1964, with Ford turning out its new product at the Dagenham plant and also in Germany. Experience with flat-fronted forward-control light commercials had convinced Baumgartner's team that the new van should have its engine located under a short bonnet, but behind a bulkhead that could contain the engine noise.

At an early stage in the proceedings, but after the design concept had been agreed (around 1963), one of the team came up with the idea that the new model could be sold to a wider audience if a chassis cab and chassis cowl version was offered. This of course was ideal for the specialist bodybuilding industry, as it meant that any amount of special adaptations could be undertaken without the need to remove or drastically alter a factory-built vehicle. By early 1964 20 prototypes (some disguised as the 400E) had been built, and a lot of night time testing was undertaken on the M2 motorway.

The introduction of the new 1.7 petrol-engined Transit in 1965 radically revolutionised the light commercial market, and although the Bedford CA still held the market share of the ice cream trade, the Transit started to make substantial inroads. In 1968 Ford began developing a 2.4 diesel engine, and in 1971 there was a switch to metric specifications. Major styling and engine changes came in 1978, and 8 years later the 'wedge' shaped Transit VE6 appeared. Today's Transit is still going strong, and in a variety of configurations it is still a very popular model in the ice cream mobiling industry. The original concept of the design team, that the new Transit should offer the same driver comforts as a car, has been progressively refined over the years giving the modern Ford almost luxury appointments when compared with the old 400E.

Top Right: *A Ford Transit MkI, fitted with the Cummins Conquest MkV for Marchetti Bros.*

Centre Right: *A MkII Transit of 1972, with a Morrison body.*

Bottom Right: *Not all Transits retained the factory fitted cowl, and some builders built their own front end. One such was Smiths of Gateshead who displayed the Cornette Seventy at the ice cream show in 1968. The large sales area, metal framing, outstanding visibility, laminated surfaces, twin wash basins and large display area were important features. Smiths were renowned for quality vehicles and their status increased even more when they took over Appleyards in early 1970. However they went out of ice cream van production soon afterwards but the firm are still active in other fields, and the Smith family operate the well-known Ringtons Tea Company who deliver door to door throughout the north. ICA*

Above: *One vehicle that we have not discussed so far is the 1962 Volkswagen 'Serve-Ice' dispenser van which employed a direct drive system from the vehicle's own engine. A caravette-style roof would lift up to give operator headroom, and the double doors opened out to show the fridge-counter, whilst a verandah canopy provided cover for the customer. Marketed by Service Garages of Colchester, the cost for a soft-ice version was £1,550 (£18,660), which compared with the £885 (£10,620) being charged for the hard-ice model with the ICI Dri-Kold freezer system. ICA*

Bottom Left: *The Bedford CA, as we have seen was long the favourite vehicle for ice cream sales and mobile food vending. Yet despite continuous improvement the CA was to suffer badly at the hands of the Transit, and in 1969 it was replaced by the new CF. However, initial problems with supply and availability was to give Bedford some problems, but the CF would eventually account for around 90% of all new mobiles. This example has a Morrison body, but turned out in the form of a mobile Fish & Chip van. When the CF2 came out in 1981 the success continued. ICA*

British Leyland Progress

The demand for more robust vehicles did not vanish altogether when the Whitby direct-drive system and the Morrison fibre-glass body came out. These two weight-saving measures encouraged many vendors to go back to the Bedford CA, but not everyone trusted the new system at first. To be fair the direct drive system did have its teething troubles, and like all new technology it was not always as reliable as it could have been during those early days. Indeed it was quite common for Bryan Whitby to work late into the night in order to get his customers back out on the road for the next day. Customer service obviously mattered, but it was also important for them to overcome the niggling little problems. Eventually all the bugs were ironed out of the system and reliability was assured, but even so personal preferences died hard.

Just as the Bedford CA had won its devotees, the Austin-Morris J series had won theirs. However the replacement J2 type 16-18cwt chassis was really not the vehicle for the mid-1960s. When you put it against the improved Bedford CA and the new Ford Transit, it was woefully antiquated. Their next model, the J4 was little better. By the mid-1960s the LDs were also getting a little long in the tooth. The problem was that the British Motor Corporation had nothing to answer the competition, although it did have a new mid-range van under development. In the meantime they had brought out the JU series in the 16-18cwt range, and in 1971 Pollocks offered the 250JU Compact for hard-ice work at a cost of £1,350 (£10,935).

The FG and EA series were developed for heavier work but the move to even heavier chassis was counterproductive for BMC, and its successor British Leyland, as it priced them far higher than the Transit and CF. However British Leyland did eventually come forward with a practical alternative to the competition, in the shape of the Austin Sherpa. Although a lively and smart looking commercial, it was prone to rust and electrical problems after a period of service and it was not always the most reliable of vehicles. Even so quite a number were used in ice cream work, and once again one of the firms offering a body were Pollocks, who advertised prices starting with a hard-ice van at £4,950 (£15,000) in 1978. At the smaller end of the scale a number of builders had used the Austin A35 and the Morris 1000 van, and the Marina-based van continued to fulfil this part of the market, but numbers were not large.

Top Right: *A Cummins-bodied BMC FG, a van which became very popular for bread delivery and parcels work in the 1960s.*

Centre Right: *The replacement for the BMC J series finally came with the BMC JU250 series in 1967 and used by a variety of operators including police forces and the Royal Mail. This example is bodied by the Scottish builders Pollock of Motherwell.* ICA

Bottom Right: *Carrying another Pollock body, we see the next development in the British Leyland range who introduced the Austin Sherpa in 1976.* ICA

Size Matters

Following on from the small 5-7cwt chassis of the 1960s, the 1970s saw a new generation of ice cream mobiles, with vehicle sizes ranging from small micro-vans through to midi-bus chassis. With the advent of the fibreglass body and a combination of traditional coachbuilding skills, it is interesting to see how the market developed in the 1970s and '80s. An interesting example of new maker seriously entering the field was Fiat. It was possibly an obvious choice for many Italian family businesses, but the fact that Fiat could supply both micro-vans and supersize machines was interesting. The advent of Japanese vehicles, like Honda, Diahatsu and Suzuki carried on the micro concept, and on to these models there was still a large number of bodybuilders with a variety of styles. With these combinations the mobiling industry had a complete range of vans, covering all sizes, prices and levels of performance and reliability. It was very much a matter of choice

Top Left: *This 1973-4 model Fiat was used by Lyons Maid in the sale of hard-ices. They were economical to purchase and the fore-runner of the micro-commercial paving the way for the Honda Acty, Bedford Rascal, Diahatsu and Suzuki models that followed.*

Centre Left: *This Fiat 55 for Izzi's Ice Creams carried much more equipment than a conventional mobile. Using a power take off to drive an alternator, as opposed to just soft-ice machines, the 'super mobile' could carry extra equipment like microwaves, milk shake machines and slush makers, etc.*

Bottom Left: *Another micro-van import was the Honda Acty and it was introduced in a mobiling version at the Bournemouth show in 1977. Although ideal for getting round narrow or congested streets they were considerably under powered and not all that stable (due to their short wheel base and narrow track), but they did do around 50 mpg.*

Right: *Using the Honda Acty chassis took mobile vending to new horizons. One of the most fascinating or grotesque (depending on your viewpoint) was the 'Uncle Sam' fibreglass body by Cummins. For those who have not made the connection, the name Uncle Sam being taken from the American patriarch Samuel Houston. The state of Texas has a city named after this great leader, but one wonders what he would think of this edifice.*

Into The Eighties & Nineties.

By the 1980s European and Japanese vehicle manufacturers were making massive in-roads into the British light commercial market, with firms like Volkswagen, Mercedes, Renault, Fiat, Honda, Suzuki, Diahatsu all gaining some measure of success at the cost of the declining British makers. British Leyland were still supplying the Sherpa, Ford were on to the MkIII Transit and Bedford had the CF. However it would not be long before Bedford went out of commercial vehicle production altogether, and it was an unhappy time for the British motor industry. Yet no one can deny the sheer versatility and reliability of the new vans that were coming into the country, despite the fact that they also had their problems, as for example the problems VW had with engine compartment fires.

In so many ways the progress in ice cream mobiling has been phenomenal, but the three key factors can be counted as:

The Soft Ice Cream Revolution
The Whitby Direct Drive System
The Morrison-Electrofreeze all-fibreglass body.

In some ways little else has changed since the mid-1960s, although considerable progress has been with the many ongoing refinements that have been added; improved equipment, better internal appointments, considerable advances in hygiene provision, and so on. In some ways the bulk of the improvements have been in advanced chassis technology, and these have been driven by the commercial vehicle industry. Therefore the improvements have been generic to the transport industry, and not specific to mobiling.

Chassis prices have impacted heavily on the cost of the ice cream mobile, and a basic Transit van now costs £13,750. Compare this with the 22cwt Transit when it was introduced in 1965 at a cost of £747 (£7,500). In 1999 a hard ice cream van based on the Transit 120 diesel will cost (£23,200) and a soft van (£32,850), however if we deduct the cost of the chassis from these prices, we can work back to what today's prices would have been in 1965. For a fully equipped hard ice cream body it would be £578 (as opposed to the price of £600 then) and £929 for a soft van body (£1,250 in 1965). So, in real terms, today's soft van is an exceptionally good deal for your lolly!

Top Right: *Along the same conceptual lines as the Fiat opposite, this Mercedes 508D offers a 'supersize' mobile. These are not so practical for local house to house vending, but ideal for large events where maximising sales potential is crucial.* ICA

Centre Right: *The slightly smaller van-based Mercedes 307D was ideal for ice cream work, as seen in this Cummins-bodied model. The Mercedes has now become a popular chassis for bodying for mobile vending, but the Bedford name has gone completely.* ICA

Bottom Right: *With the demise of Bedford it was understandable that the Transit would get a lion's share of the mobile market and as Ford tell us, the Transit has become 'The Backbone of Britain. Nestle obviously agree and this carries the company's latest branding*

Mind That Child

For as long as there have been ice cream vans, there has been the danger of eager youngsters dashing into the road to get to their much-loved treat, blissfully unaware of the dangers of the road that separates them from their 'bounty'. When a child gets unfortunately injured in this way, the press often have a field day with the tragic mobiler and the industry in general. For example headlines of 1963 and 1964 in particular talked of 'potential hazards', 'dangers to children', and 'parking dangers'.

For example *The Wolverhampton Express & Star* asked for 'Care with Cornets', after Halesowen's road safety committee asked van operators to 'sell road safety as they sell ice cream'. In February 1964 *The Peterborough Standard* reported an alarming rise in accidents, with children under the age of five being the most likely to be hit. It went on to assert that, more often than not, children were killed in accidents where ice cream vans were operating. Brighton Teachers' Association even suggested the vans themselves were the danger, with some drivers said to be parking outside the school gates and waiting for the kids to leave their studies for the day, then racing off to another school - and then back to the first for when the older children headed home. No-parking lines outside school gates were one option being considered, special lighting for the vans themselves was another.

Yet was all this criticism of the ice cream van accurate or fair? Well before these criticisms the Royal Society for the Prevention of Accidents (RoSPA), had expressed concern at the general increase in accidents involving children as road vehicles grew in numbers. In 1962 they launched a campaign - and the Tufty Club - in conjunction with local authorities, road safety officials and accident prevention councils. They also approached ice cream van operators asking them to display 'Stop - Look Before Crossing' posters. Clearly RoSPA recognised that ice cream vans were not only a potential source of danger, but a valuable asset in getting across the road safety message. Using characters with the names of Lollipop Larry and Cornet Katie, this was a valuable part of Road Training Year. It also featured the look right - look left campaign, which had been devised to cut down on general accidents.

The ice cream campaign was designed to remind youngsters of the dangers of stepping out from behind the ice cream van into the traffic. The posters were complimented with dashboard notices telling drivers to watch out for children before moving off. Parents were also advised to supervise their young ones on trips to the ice cream van. Later, vans had to display large "Mind that Child" signs (many illuminated from within) at their backs to warn oncoming motorists.

Top Left: *This wonderful picture of a Cummins-bodied Bedford CA shows that firms like Stevens Ices were quite aware of the potential dangers to children. It is clearly adopting the road safety slogan of the late-1950s, Look Right - Look Left!*

Top Right: *Adopting a different tactic, this Commer 1-ton with a Cummins body, aims its message at oncoming drivers by using a 'painted policeman'. Supplied to Deal Beach Parlours in Kent, this van is pictured outside a Rootes Service garage.*

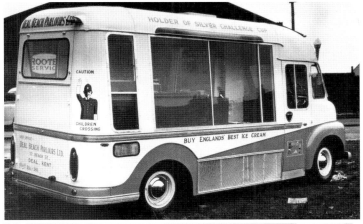

Centre Right: *An example of an elaborate 'Mind That Child' panel at the back of a Cummins bodied Bedford CF.* ICA

Bottom Right: *When we were compiling this book, it occurred to the authors that not only had the British ice cream industry done much to protect its young clientele, but it had also exported the road safety message worldwide. An example of our Mind That Child campaign is clearly illustrated on this Cummins-bodied Ford Transit supplied to Holland.*

By the summer of 1966, RoSPA and the Ice Cream Alliance had Bryan Whitby produce a 'fleet' of around 25 miniature ice cream vans, which were to be used in safety campaigns and road safety drills around the country. These went to places as diverse as Wandsworth in London and Kendal in Westmorland. Kids were able to ride around in them whilst still learning road sense and dangers. By the summer of 1970 the Ice Cream Federation, the Ice Cream Alliance, and RoSPA had produced a colour safety film to help generate safety awareness. This film depicted two children heading out of their front garden and watching for traffic as they headed for the ice cream van to buy their favourite ices; this was generally agreed to have been 'well-prepared and would serve a useful purpose.' Much more has been accomplished in the years that have followed, and the latest improvement are rear-looking cameras that show drivers what is going on behind their van.

The problem of excited (but more importantly, unsupervised children) running across the road to spend their pocket money will always be with us. Yet the industry has done much to prevent the danger and create a public awareness, but how many car drivers really anticipate the danger as they run down a road where an ice cream van may be standing. Recent campaigns such as 'kill your speed not a child' advocate a maximum speed of 20mph in built-up residential areas', but do we always remember this? Similarly we as parents should always be mindful about controlling our children when they go out to buy ice creams, in other words we must keep our eye on them at all times. In conclusion, if this short section of our book has made you think about the potential dangers of children around ice cream vans, it has been worth our including it. Remember, we will only know about those accidents that sadly happen, never the ones that we have prevented. It rests upon us all to keep to the maxim, PREVENTION IS BETTER THAN THE CURE!

Above: *This Bedford CF2 was an interesting experiment which, whilst never taking off at the time, should (perhaps) be a prototype for the future. Working with Bedford, General Motors and Lucas, the bodybuilder Robin Hood (who had acquired Morrisons by this time) built 'The All-Electric Ice Cream Van'. Only a few of the electric Bedford CFs were built in 1983-4, but the bus version was used by HRH Prince Philip as a shooting brake. This one carries slogans that read Payload 10.19kgs (including driver), No road fund licence fees, No MOT annual test required, 50% less maintenance costs and 2.2 year warranty.* ICA

ACKNOWLEDGMENTS

Roy Aitken
Bill Aldridge
Alistair Aynscough
Robert Berry
BMC Owners Club
Bedford CA Owners Club
Birds Eye - Walls
Stuart Birkby
Josef Boni
Don Brennan
Dudley Brierley

Tony Colletta
Tony Connor
David Cummins
Ade Davies
Paul Dickson
Kevin & Margaret Donovan
Graham Ellis
FIAT
Lisa Greene
Ford of Great Britain
Harvin Chimes

HCVS
Hocking's Ice Cream
Ice Cream Alliance
Andrew Neilson
Mercedes Benz
Nestle
Barry Older
Steve Pheasant
Peugot-Talbot
Rover Cars plc
Gerald Ryan

Dennis Sherer
Slees Ice Cream
University of Guelph
University of Philadelphia
University of York
Vauxhall Motors Ltd.
Volkswagen
Eustace Voght
Barry Walker
R Weir
Barry Woods